ALICANTE

CHRISTMAS

Travel Guide 2023

Festive Fun in the City of Alicante, Your

Spain Christmas, New Year and

Festivals Season 2023 Itinerary

Thomas A. Olvera

Table of Contents

1. INTRODUCTION

1.1 Welcome to Alicante: The Christmas City

During the holiday season, Alicante, also known as the "Christmas City," comes alive with festive charm. When you enter this Spanish jewel for your 2023 Christmas and New Year's celebrations, you'll be greeted by a distinct and enchanting environment that distinguishes it from other options. This travel guide will help you discover the enchantment of Alicante during this festive season.

1.2 Overview of Alicante

Alicante, on Spain's eastern coast in the province of Alicante, is a coastal city famed for its beautiful beaches, rich history, and active culture. The city is set between the Mediterranean Sea and the magnificent mountains, providing visitors with a broad choice of experiences. Its unique combination of natural beauty and cultural legacy makes it a year-round destination.

1.3 History and Culture

Alicante's history includes a patchwork of influences from the Iberians, Romans, Moors, and Christians weaved over centuries. The heritage of the city can be seen in its architecture, traditions, and festivals. Alicante's Christmas celebrations are strongly steeped in these historical and cultural influences, making it a one-of-a-kind and unforgettable experience for tourists.

1.4 Geography and Climate

Alicante, located in Spain's Costa Blanca region, has a Mediterranean climate. This guarantees warm winters and bright skies, especially throughout the holidays. The natural beauty of the city is highlighted by its beaches, especially the famed Postiguet Beach, and the majestic Mount Benacantil, which is home to the old Santa Bárbara Castle. The combination of sea and mountain gives an unforgettable setting for your Christmas break.

1.5 Why Choose Alicante for Your 2023 Festive Season?

You may be wondering what distinguishes Alicante as a destination for your Christmas and New Year's celebrations. The explanation lies in the city's distinct blend of heritage, celebration, and modernization. Residents in Alicante enjoy the Christmas season wholeheartedly, and the city is decked out in sparkling lights, nativity scenes, and festive decorations. During this unique time of year, the warm and welcoming ambiance will make you feel right at home.

Furthermore, due to its location on the Mediterranean coast, Alicante has a warm winter temperature, making it a great destination for people looking for a sun-filled break during the holiday season. While much of Europe is shivering in the cold, you may bask in the Mediterranean sun while seeing the city's cultural riches and savoring wonderful Spanish food.

1.6 Quick Overview of Your Itinerary

I have created an itinerary that combines tradition, entertainment, and discovery to help you make the most of your Alicante Christmas vacation. Your days in Alicante will be jam-packed with activities that highlight the finest of the city's culture and holiday atmosphere. Here's a quick rundown of what to expect throughout your stay:

Day 1: Arrival and City Orientation

- Arrive in Alicante and check into your chosen lodging.

- Take a stroll down the gorgeous Explanada de España.

- Dine at a local restaurant for a traditional Spanish lunch.

Day 2: Exploring the Old Town

- Immerse yourself in Alicante's history by touring the city's lovely old town, Barrio Santa Cruz.

- Visit Santa Bárbara Castle for panoramic city views.

- Visit the Santa Maria Basilica and the San Nicolás Co-Cathedral.

Day 3: Christmas Markets and Culinary Delights

- Visit the crowded Christmas markets, such as the Mercado de Navidad, and browse for one-of-a-kind presents and decorations.

- Indulge in the delights of Alicante's Christmas gastronomy, which includes traditional dishes like Turron and Polvorones.

- In the evening, go to a Christmas concert or performance.

Day 4: New Year's Eve Celebrations

- Plan a special dinner at a local restaurant for a memorable New Year's Eve.

- Join the jubilant crowds on the streets as they ring in the new year with fireworks and celebrations.

- For an unforgettable night, visit the numerous bars and clubs.

Day 5: Epiphany Parade and Departure

- On January 5th, see the exciting Three Kings Parade (Cabalgata de los Reyes Magos).

- Take part in the celebration of Epiphany, the day of presenting gifts.

- Say goodbye to Alicante and embark on your next adventure.

As you go across Alicante, you will experience the beauty of its traditions, the kindness of its people, and the magic of Christmas in a one-of-a-kind setting. This travel book will give you in-depth insights, practical suggestions, and recommendations to make your holiday season in Alicante unforgettable and magical. So, prepare to open the present of an extraordinary Christmas in the Christmas City.

2. PLANNING YOUR TRIP

2.1 Best Time to Visit Alicante for Christmas

Choosing the best time to visit Alicante for your Christmas vacation is critical to making the most of your visit. The festive season in Alicante usually starts in early December and lasts until the first week of January. During this time, the city is magnificently decked, and there are numerous Christmas markets and festivities. The following are important dates to remember:

1. Early December: The city begins to deck itself out in festive decorations, and the Christmas markets open. It's a perfect opportunity to get into the holiday spirit before the throngs arrive.

2. Christmas Week: From the 24th to the 26th of December, you'll be immersed in the Spanish traditions of Nochebuena (Christmas Eve) and Navidad (Christmas Day). Because these are family-oriented celebrations, many businesses and restaurants may be closed. The city's plazas and streets, on the other hand, come alive with nativity scenes, lights, and music.

3. New Year's Eve: The 31st of December is a bustling night in Alicante. As the new year approaches, expect fireworks, parties, and street celebrations.

4. Epiphany (Día de los Reyes): The coming of the Three Kings on January 5th and 6th is a prominent holiday in Spain. Parades are held

around the city, and it's a perfect chance to see Spanish traditions.

Your preferences will determine the perfect time to visit Alicante for Christmas. Consider arriving in early December for a quieter, more intimate encounter. Plan your travel accordingly for a colorful New Year's celebration. Be aware that some services may be restricted over the Christmas and New Year's holidays, so plan your activities and dining options ahead of time.

2.2 Visa and Travel Requirements

Before traveling to Alicante for your Christmas break, make sure you have all of the appropriate travel documents. For visits of up to 90 days, most visitors to Spain, including those from the United

States, Canada, the European Union, and many other countries, do not need a visa. However, depending on your nationality and the purpose of your travel, you must check the specific visa requirements. Check that your passport is valid for at least six months after your intended travel date.

Travel insurance is also highly recommended, as it covers you for unforeseen circumstances like trip cancellations, medical problems, and lost luggage. Examine your insurance policy's terms and conditions to ensure you have appropriate coverage for your Christmas holiday.

2.3 Communication and Internet Access

It is critical to stay connected while in Alicante for navigation, communication, and sharing your experiences. Thankfully, the city provides dependable communication and internet connections. Here are some suggestions for staying connected:

1. SIM Cards: When you arrive, consider getting a local SIM card. Prepaid solutions including data and voice bundles are available from major providers such as Movistar, Vodafone, and Orange. This will ensure that you have an internet connection and can make local calls as needed.

2. Wi-Fi: The majority of Alicante's hotels, restaurants, and cafes offer free Wi-Fi to their customers. These connections can help you save money on data.

3. Mobile Apps: To explore the city more efficiently, download handy travel apps such as Google Maps, translation apps, and local transit apps.

2.4 Getting There

Alicante is well-connected to major cities in Europe and beyond, making it accessible to visitors from all over the world. The following are the principal modes of transportation for getting to Alicante:

1. Alicante-Elche Airport (ALC) is the closest airport to Alicante and provides both domestic and international flights. You may easily access the city center by taxi, bus, or tram from the airport.

2. Train: Alicante Train Station connects the city to Spain's large railway network, providing access to important cities such as Madrid and Barcelona.

3. Long-distance buses are another alternative for getting to Alicante from neighboring towns and countries. Bus services are both efficient and cost-effective.

4. Car: If you want to go by car, you can do it at the airport or in the city. Spain's road infrastructure is well-maintained, and driving from big cities like Valencia and Murcia is simple.

To obtain the best costs and ensure availability, it's better to schedule your transportation in advance, especially during the holiday season. Remember that some flights or itineraries may be more limited over the Christmas season, so plan accordingly.

2.5 Accommodation Options

Alicante has a variety of housing alternatives to suit all budgets and preferences. During the Christmas season, it is best to book your accommodations ahead of time to guarantee your preferred dates. Consider the following sorts of lodging:

1. Hotels: Alicante has a wide range of hotels to select from, including luxury resorts, boutique hotels, and budget-friendly options. Stay in the city center to be close to the Christmas activities.

2. Consider hiring a vacation apartment or villa for a more spacious and private stay. These alternatives are ideal for larger groups or families.

3. Hostels: If you're traveling on a budget, various hostels in Alicante offer both dormitories and individual rooms.

4. Bed and Breakfasts: Staying in a B&B allows you to experience local hospitality while learning about the city's Christmas traditions.

5. Resorts: If you want to have a deluxe experience, book a resort near the beach where you can relax and enjoy the holiday season.

Your lodging options will be determined by your budget, group size, and personal preferences. Make sure your lodging is centrally positioned so that you can easily access the city's Christmas markets, sights, and festivities.

2.6 Budgeting for Your Christmas Vacation

Creating a budget for your Christmas vacation in Alicante is vital for efficiently managing your costs. Here is a summary of prospective costs to think about:

1. Accommodation: Plan ahead of time and arrange your lodging. Prices vary according to location, room type, and availability.

2. Plan for flights, rail tickets, or other modes of transportation to and from Alicante. You should also budget for local transportation within the city.

3. Spend money on meals at local restaurants, traditional Spanish cuisine, and seasonal goodies. Remember to try some of Alicante's Christmas treats.

4. Activities and Entertainment: Budget for excursions, admission fees, and tickets to Christmas activities and shows.

5. Shopping: The Christmas markets in Alicante provide one-of-a-kind items and decorations. Include a shopping budget for celebration souvenirs.

6. Emergency Funds: Set aside some money for unforeseen bills or emergencies.

7. Travel Insurance: Include the cost of travel insurance in your budget to guarantee you're protected in the event of an emergency.

If you aren't using the euro, keep an eye on currency conversion rates and notify your bank of your vacation intentions to avoid problems when using your credit or debit card abroad.

2.7 Packing Tips for a Winter and Festive Holiday

Packing for your Christmas vacation in Alicante necessitates taking into account the winter weather as well as the festive festivities. Here are some must-have products for your packing list:

1. Pack warm layers, such as sweaters, coats, and scarves, as the nights can be chilly. Walking shoes that are comfortable are essential for visiting the city.

2. Bring a few dressier outfits for holiday celebrations and New Year's Eve celebrations. During the holiday season, many restaurants and events encourage people to dress up.

3. Ensure you have the correct adapters to charge your electronic gadgets in Spain. The standard voltage is 230 volts, with a frequency of 50 hertz.

4. Consider investing in a simple Spanish phrasebook or a translation app to aid conversation. While English is widely spoken in

Alicante, locals value efforts to speak their language.

5. Camera and Accessories: Use your camera or smartphone to capture the enchantment of Christmas in Alicante. Remember to include spare memory cards and charging connections.

6. Bring any necessary prescriptions as well as a tiny first-aid kit for minor health emergencies.

7. Keep your passport, travel insurance information, flight tickets, and hotel bookings in a safe, easily accessible location.

8. Reusable Shopping Bag: Because you'll be lured by the unusual things at the Christmas markets, a reusable shopping bag comes in handy.

9. Umbrella: While Alicante has a mild winter, rain showers do occur on occasion.

You'll be well-prepared to enjoy your Christmas vacation in Alicante if you pack sensibly and consider both the weather and the seasonal celebrations. Check the weather forecast closer to your departure date to fine-tune your packing list.

3. EXPLORING ALICANTE

3.1 Overview of Alicante's Attractions

Alicante is a city that successfully combines modern conveniences with a rich historical history. Exploring its attractions during the Christmas season is a joyous occasion. Here's a rundown of some of the must-see attractions:

1. Santa Barbara Castle: Perched atop Mount Benacantil, this landmark castle provides panoramic views of the city and ocean. The castle, which dates back to the 9th century, is ideal for history buffs and photographers both.

2. Explanada de España: Take a stroll along this palm-lined promenade. With street artists, cafes,

and marketplaces, it's a hive of activity. It is decked out with Christmas lights and ornaments, creating a lovely ambiance.

3. Explore the Basilica of Santa Maria, a beautiful specimen of Gothic architecture in Alicante's old town. The 14th-century basilica is not just a place of prayer but also an architectural wonder with meticulous detailing.

4. San Juan Beach: While the winter sun isn't ideal for sunbathing, San Juan Beach is worth a visit for its peace and beauty. Enjoy the pleasant Mediterranean climate by taking a peaceful walk along the beach.

3.2 Must-Visit Christmas Markets

The Christmas markets in Alicante are a treasure trove of festive energy, local crafts, and delectable delights. Here are a few markets that should be on your list:

1. Mercado de Navidad: This historic Christmas market in the city center sells a wide range of presents, decorations, and seasonal cuisine. Don't pass up the opportunity to enjoy "Turron," a traditional Christmas dessert in Spain.

2. Market Plaza de Gabriel Miró: This market is well-known for its artistic and artisanal wares. It's the ideal place to find one-of-a-kind, handcrafted presents and ornaments for your loved ones.

3. The Mercado de Belén specializes in nativity scenes, which are an important aspect of Spanish Christmas traditions. To make your nativity display, you can select intricately sculpted figurines and accessories.

4. Mercado de Reyes: This market comes alive around Epiphany, Spain's day of gift-giving. It's a vibrant, bustling market where you can find the ideal gifts for your friends and family.

Exploring these marketplaces helps you to get into the holiday spirit while also bringing back authentic Spanish Christmas goods.

3.3 Touring the Historic Old Town

Barrio Santa Cruz, Alicante's historic old town, is a tangle of narrow streets, colorful buildings, and charming squares. Exploring this quaint neighborhood is like going back in time. Here's what to expect:

1. San Nicolás Co-Cathedral: See this gorgeous co-cathedral with its elaborate baroque elements and outstanding murals. It's a tranquil spot to take in the city's history and architecture.

2. Stroll through the Santa Cruz area, which is famed for its lovely white cottages and vivid bougainvillea. It's a scenic place that's especially lovely during the holiday season.

3. Museo de Arte del Siglo XX (MACA): If you enjoy art, the MACA is a must-see. It is home to an impressive collection of twentieth-century art, including pieces by local artists.

4. Tapas Bars and Cafes: There are various tapas bars and cafes around the old town. Take a break and enjoy some Spanish tapas or a cup of hot chocolate, which are ideal for keeping warm in the winter.

3.4 A Day at the Beach: Alicante's Winter Sunshine

While Alicante's beaches are most popular in the summer, they have a special allure in the winter. San Juan Beach, in particular, is a great place to spend a relaxed day by the sea. The mild

Mediterranean temperature allows for enjoyable walks along the beach, and the views of the sea and city are equally enthralling in winter.

You can take a stroll, collect seashells, or simply relax and enjoy the tranquil atmosphere. Many beachside cafés and restaurants are still open, allowing you to enjoy fresh seafood or a steaming cup of Spanish hot chocolate with churros. Because of the lack of summer crowds, you can have the beach all to yourself, making it an ideal area for reflection and relaxation.

During the winter season, Alicante's unique blend of historical charm, bustling Christmas markets, and the attractiveness of its beaches provides a genuinely wonderful experience. You'll be able to appreciate the city's uniqueness and make the most

of your Christmas vacation in Alicante if you visit
these attractions.

4. FESTIVE CELEBRATION

4.1 Christmas Traditions in Alicante

Alicante, a city rich in tradition, celebrates Christmas with a distinct blend of local traditions and global holiday rituals. Understanding these traditions will enhance your Christmas vacation experience. Some of Alicante's most treasured Christmas traditions include:

1. Nativity Scenes or Belén: The nativity scene, or "Belén" in Spanish, is an important feature of Christmas celebrations. Nativity scenes are shown in public areas across Alicante, including churches and town centers. These complex dioramas, typically with painstaking attention to detail, reflect the biblical story of Jesus' birth.

2. Misa del Gallo (Rooster's Mass): Attending Midnight Mass on Christmas Eve is a beloved Alicante tradition. Misa del Gallo, or Rooster's Mass, is celebrated in churches throughout the city. It is a time for thought, prayer, and celebration of Jesus' birth.

3. Nochebuena and Christmas Eve Dinner: On Christmas Eve, Spanish families meet for a joyful feast known as "Nochebuena," which includes traditional foods such as roast lamb, seafood, and desserts such as "Turron" and "Polvorones." The evening is defined by warmth, community, and the exchanging of presents.

4. Christmas Day Celebrations: Christmas Day in Alicante is a more relaxed, family-oriented affair. Many businesses and restaurants may be closed as

residents spend time with family and friends. Nativity figures, bright lights, and music fill the streets.

5. New Year's Eve customs include eating 12 grapes at midnight, in addition to the traditional countdown and fireworks. Each grape symbolizes good fortune for one month of the following year.

4.2 Attending Midnight Mass

Attending the Midnight Mass, or Misa del Gallo, if you're in Alicante for Christmas, is a profound and culturally stimulating experience. This special ceremony, held in many churches throughout the city, brings the community together to commemorate the birth of Jesus. The mood is peaceful, and the churches' interiors are decked out with traditional Christmas decorations such as nativity scenes and festive lighting.

The Midnight Mass is held in Alicante's historic churches, such as the Co-cathedral of San Nicolás and the Basilica of Santa Mara. Hymns, prayers, and a retelling of the nativity story are frequently included in the Mass. It's a chance to experience the spiritual side of the Christmas season while also immersing oneself in the local culture.

Attending Midnight Mass is both a religious and cultural tradition in Alicante. Whether you're a devout Christian or simply interested in local customs, this experience can be a poignant and real way to celebrate Christmas in Alicante.

4.3 New Year's Eve in Alicante

In Alicante, New Year's Eve, known as "Nochevieja" in Spanish, is widely celebrated. If you're in town for New Year's Eve, you can expect a night full of excitement and tradition. Here's how Alicante is ringing in the new year:

1. Fireworks: As the clock strikes midnight, a dazzling display of fireworks illuminates the city. Locals and visitors alike assemble in plazas and along the Explanada de España to watch this spectacular show. The explosion of colors in the night sky heralds the start of a new year.

2. 12 Grapes: It is typical to eat 12 grapes as the clock approaches midnight, one with each chime of the clock. Each grape symbolizes good fortune

for one month of the following year. This is a custom that practically everyone in Spain observes, and it is often savored in front of the television as the clock tower of Puerta del Sol in Madrid strikes midnight.

3. New Year's Eve Parties: Many Alicante restaurants, pubs, and clubs offer New Year's Eve parties. These gatherings frequently feature live music, dancing, and beautiful décor. It's a terrific way to ring in the new year in a fun and festive atmosphere.

4. Dress to Impress: Because Spaniards frequently dress up for New Year's Eve events, consider wearing your nicest outfit. For good luck, many locals wear something red.

In Alicante, New Year's Eve is a night of joy, contemplation, and the promise of a new beginning. It's a time to join the local community in toasting the end of the old year and ushering in the new one with optimism and joy.

4.4 Epiphany and the Three Kings Parade

The Epiphany, or "Día de los Reyes," is one of Spain's most important and celebrated holidays. It commemorates the appearance of the Three Wise Men (Los Reyes Magos), who gave gifts to the infant Jesus. The Epiphany is celebrated in Alicante with a lively parade known as the "Cabalgata de los Reyes Magos."

This spectacular procession winds its way through the streets of Alicante on January 5th, featuring colorful floats carrying the Three Kings and their entourages. Children look forward to the parade since it is the day they receive their gifts, similar to Christmas morning in other nations.

The parade is a musical, dancing, and costume extravaganza. The Three Kings shower the people with candy and tiny gifts, making it a happy moment for families and children. People of all ages have gathered to celebrate this beloved custom, creating an electrifying atmosphere.

The Three Kings Parade and the Epiphany provide a unique look into Spanish culture and the significance of the holiday season. As you watch this exciting event, you will not only be immersed in Alicante's festive mood, but you will also develop a greater appreciation for the traditions that make the city's Christmas celebrations so remarkable.

5. ENTERTAINMENT AND EVENTS

5.1 Festive Concerts and Shows

During the Christmas season, Alicante comes alive with a variety of festive concerts and shows. These events combine traditional Spanish music with contemporary acts and appealing spectacles. Attending these concerts and shows is an excellent way to get into the holiday spirit. Here are a few examples:

1. Christmas Concerts: Many Alicante churches and cultural centers organize Christmas concerts featuring choirs, orchestras, and solo musicians. These concerts frequently incorporate a blend of

classical and traditional Spanish music, resulting in a wonderful environment that embodies the essence of the season.

2. Flamenco Performances: Experience the passion and fire of Flamenco, a traditional Spanish art form. Flamenco presentations that feature holiday themes are available during the Christmas season, giving a unique and festive touch on this mesmerizing dance and music style.

3. Theater Productions: The theaters in Alicante present a range of holiday-themed plays and events. These can range from family-friendly plays, such as retellings of classic Christmas tales, to more avant-garde acts that inject artistic expression into the holiday season.

4. Cultural activities: Look for cultural activities that honor Alicante's legacy. These can include exhibitions, art installations, and performances that represent the city's Christmas history and traditions.

5. Christmas Caroling: Take advantage of the opportunity to participate in or listen to local caroling events. Carolers are frequently seen wandering the streets and plazas, serenading passers-by with traditional Christmas carols. It's a touching experience that adds a sense of community and togetherness to the holiday season.

Check event listings and local marketing for a calendar of Christmas concerts and events taking place during your visit. Attending these concerts is a fantastic way to make long-lasting holiday memories in Alicante.

5.2 Fireworks and Light Displays

Alicante's Christmas season is defined by fireworks and light shows. The city is adorned with spectacular decorations and brilliant shows that give the nights a sense of magic and awe. Here's what to expect:

1. Fireworks on New Year's Eve: As the clock strikes midnight on New Year's Eve, Alicante puts on a stunning fireworks show. Locals and visitors alike assemble in plazas and along the Explanada de Espana to watch this spectacular show. The explosion of colors in the night sky marks the start of a new year and is a time of joy and celebration.

2. Christmas Lights: Alicante's streets and buildings are decked out in lovely Christmas lights throughout December and early January. Stroll through the city center to view the exquisite displays that give the urban landscape a festive glow.

3. Nativity Scene Illuminations: Many of Alicante's nativity scenes, or "Belenes," are complemented by elaborate lighting and sound effects that enhance the storyline. These illuminated images are frequently seen in churches, plazas, and public places.

4. Light Shows: Dedicated light shows synchronized to music are held in several places in the city. These enthralling spectacles create a fantastic ambiance and are frequently

accompanied by street performances and entertainment.

5. Beach Fireworks: If you go to the beach, you may see smaller, unplanned fireworks displays put on by locals. These unexpected performances offer a magical touch to your winter coastal experience.

The mix of fireworks and light shows lends grandeur and festivity to the Christmas celebrations in Alicante. Whether it's ringing in the new year with a bang or soaking in the warmth of the city's holiday lights, these displays add to the season's particular charm.

5.3 Christmas-Themed Activities for Kids

During the Christmas season, Alicante is a family-friendly destination with a variety of events geared to amuse children of all ages. Here are some festive activities that kids will love:

1. Visit Santa Claus: There are several Santa Claus places in Alicante where youngsters can see him and share their Christmas wishes. Many children look forward to sitting on Santa's lap and telling him about their wishes.

2. Nativity Scene Workshops: In Alicante, children can construct their small nativity scenes. These workshops not only provide a pleasant and instructive experience for children, but they also

teach them about the importance of the nativity scene in Spanish Christmas traditions.

3. Children's entertainment: Alicante's theaters frequently present family-friendly Christmas entertainment such as plays, puppet shows, and musicals. These events are ideal for a festive family adventure during the holidays.

4. Outdoor Ice Skating: Temporary outdoor ice rinks are set up in various areas across Alicante, giving children an exciting ice-skating experience. Skates can be rented, and this sport is a great combination of winter enjoyment and workout.

5. Parades and Festivals: For children, the Three Kings Parade, or "Cabalgata de los Reyes Magos," is a highlight. The colorful floats, characters, and

sweets distribution make it a fun event. Other parades and festive events are also planned with children's enjoyment in mind.

6. Chocolate con Churros: Treat your children to a delightful and warming cup of Spanish hot chocolate, which is frequently served with churros, a popular local food.

Christmas-themed activities for children in Alicante bring a sense of wonder and enchantment to the season, creating lasting memories for the entire family. These activities ensure that children have a fantastic holiday experience in Christmas City, whether it's greeting Santa, constructing nativity scenes, or ice skating.

6. OUTDOOR ACTIVITIES

6.1 Hiking in the Alicante Mountains

While Christmas in Alicante is traditionally linked with festive parties, the surrounding countryside allows outdoor enthusiasts to explore the gorgeous Alicante Mountains. This is a good alternative for people looking to get away from the city's hustle and bustle. Here are several hikes to consider for a wonderful outdoor adventure:

1. Sierra de Aitana: The Sierra de Aitana is Alicante's highest peak, affording stunning panoramic views of the surrounding landscape. Several trails go to the peak, with routes appropriate for both expert and novice hikers. It's a

peaceful retreat into nature, especially during the quieter winter months.

2. Puig Campana: Another hiking gem in the Alicante region is Puig Campana. The trails leading to the mountain are noted for their difficult terrain, making it a popular destination for experienced hikers. The reward at the top is a 360-degree view of the countryside, which is especially lovely in the winter.

3. Serra Gelada Natural Park: For those who love seaside views, the Serra Gelada Natural Park offers a one-of-a-kind trekking experience. Its routes combine natural beauty, historical attractions, and breathtaking views of the Mediterranean Sea. You can explore paths that are appropriate for different levels of fitness.

4. Hiking in the Old Town: For a unique hiking experience, go through Alicante's ancient Old Town. The winding, small alleyways and lovely staircases provide for a great urban trekking trip, with historical and architectural landmarks to uncover along the way.

Before beginning a hiking expedition, remember to check the weather and route conditions, especially during the winter season. If you're inexperienced with the trails, dress correctly, bring water, snacks, and a map, and consider taking a guided trek.

6.2 Watersports in Winter

Even during the holiday season, Alicante's pleasant winter environment allows for a variety of watersports and outdoor activities. The Mediterranean Sea remains quite warm, allowing for watersports such as:

1. Windsurfing and Kitesurfing: The Alicante coastline is well-known for its good wind conditions, which draw windsurfers and kitesurfers all year. Experienced surfers may attack the waves, while newbies can get started with lessons.

2. Sailing: Take a sailing trip around the Mediterranean. Private charters and group sailing tours are available. The winter months provide calmer waters and a more tranquil backdrop for sailing.

3. Kayaking: Paddle along the coast, discovering hidden bays and taking in the Mediterranean scenery. Kayaking is a fun and peaceful watersport for people of all ages.

4. Scuba Diving: Alicante's underwater realm is filled with marine life and exciting dive spots. Many diving operations provide excursions for divers of various skill levels. The winter season frequently provides clean waters and enhanced visibility.

5. Snorkeling is a great approach to observing the underwater world if you prefer to stay near the surface. The seas off the coast of Alicante are ideal for snorkeling.

6. Beach Volleyball and Beach Soccer: Even in the winter, Alicante's beaches are a hotspot for beach sports. Play beach volleyball or beach soccer with your buddies and fellow guests.

To guarantee a safe and enjoyable experience, verify local legislation and safety guidelines for watersports, and consider arranging activities through trustworthy operators.

6.3 Day Trips to Nearby Towns

The strategic location of Alicante along the Costa Blanca makes it a great starting point for exploring adjacent towns and cities, each with its distinct charm and attractions. Here are some local day trip destinations to consider:

1. Elche is a UNESCO World Heritage site known for its beautiful palm grove. Visit the Elche Palmeral Museum and the exquisite Huerto del Cura Park while exploring the historic town.

2. Guadalest: A lovely castle located on a rock overlooking the valley may be seen in this picturesque mountain community. The town has breathtaking views, beautiful shops, and the opportunity to visit historic museums.

3. Altea is well-known for its lovely Old Town, where you can stroll along cobblestone alleyways, see the unique blue-domed cathedral, and dine on Mediterranean food in local eateries.

4. Villajoyosa is a charming seaside village known for its colorful buildings along the waterfront.

Explore its lively alleys, pay a visit to the Valor Chocolate Museum, and unwind on its sandy beaches.

5. Jávea (Xàbia) is well-known for its natural beauty, which includes clean beaches, coves, and the famed Montgó mountain. The Old Town is attractive, and there are excellent dining options along the beach promenade.

6. Denia: This historic coastal town has a castle, lovely beaches, and a bustling fishing harbor. It also serves as a gateway to the Balearic Islands, giving it an ideal starting place for island-hopping excursions.

These adjacent towns and cities provide a wide range of experiences, ranging from cultural discovery to natural beauty. Day tours from Alicante offer a variety of possibilities to suit your interests, whether you're interested in history, food, or simply enjoying the lovely landscapes. Make the most of your stay in this fascinating location by planning your trips accordingly.

7. CULINARY DELIGHTS

7.1 Sampling Alicante's Christmas Cuisine

Alicante's food scene is a treasure trove of flavors and customs, and it is especially delicious during the Christmas season. Here's a taste of what you may try during your Christmas break in Alicante, ranging from deep and hearty stews to sweet and indulgent treats:

1. Turron: No Christmas visit to Alicante is complete without sampling Turron, a typical Spanish nougat made from honey, sugar, and toasted almonds. It is available in a variety of tastes, including soft, hard, and chocolate-covered. This popular holiday treat can be found in local shops and marketplaces.

2. Roscón de Reyes: This ring-shaped cake is a traditional Epiphany treat in Spain. The Roscón de Reyes is frequently decorated with candied fruits and conceals miniature figurines and a fava bean. The finder of the figurines is thought to have good luck, whilst the finder of the fava bean is required to pay for the cake the next year.

3. Pavo Trufado: Pavo Trufado, a dish of turkey roasted with truffles and a thick sauce, is a popular Christmas food in Alicante. The earthy aroma of truffles combined with juicy turkey is a wonderful holiday pleasure.

4. Coques: Coques are savory pastries that differ by area in Spain. Coca de Mollitas, a crispy dough topped with little bits of salted fish, olives, and

tomatoes, may be found in Alicante. These pastries are a filling and savory snack.

5. Gambas al Ajillo: Shrimp sautéed in olive oil with garlic and chili flakes in this traditional Spanish dish. The sizzling, fragrant tastes of Gambas al Ajillo are a popular holiday snack.

7.2 Traditional Spanish Dishes

During the Christmas season, you'll find classic Spanish meals that are strongly ingrained in the country's culture when discovering Alicante's gastronomic wonders. Here are a few traditional Spanish foods you should try:

1. Paella: While Paella Valenciana is traditionally associated with the Valencia region, it is also

available in Alicante. It's a hearty and savory option made with saffron-seasoned rice and a variety of proteins like chicken, rabbit, veggies, and shellfish.

2. Pulpo a la Gallega: Tender octopus slices drizzled with olive oil, paprika, and salt make this Galician-style octopus a delectable appetizer. It's a simple but tasty dish that's frequently served throughout the holiday season.

3. Jamon Iberico: Spain is famous for its cured hams, and Jamon Iberico is an absolute must-try. It's created from Iberian pigs fed on acorns and matured to perfection, resulting in a melt-in-your-mouth pleasure.

4. Gazpacho: While gazpacho is more typically associated with the summer months, it is also popular in Alicante during the winter. This chilled tomato-based soup with garlic, peppers, and other fresh vegetables is a pleasant alternative to heartier holiday meals.

5. Churros con Chocolate: Churros are a popular Spanish dessert, especially around the holidays. Deep-fried dough pastries are frequently served with a cup of thick, creamy hot chocolate for dipping. It's a delectable dessert or a decadent brunch alternative.

7.3 Must-Try Christmas Treats

Aside from the traditional food, there are a few Christmas delicacies you must taste while in

Alicante. These sweet and savory treats encapsulate the flavor of the Spanish holiday season:

1. Polvorones: These flaky, almond-based shortbread cookies are a Christmas tradition in Spain. They are frequently accompanied by a cup of coffee or a glass of sweet wine.

2. Mantecados: Another favorite Christmas cookie in Spain is mantecados. These soft and crumbly pastries are frequently scented with cinnamon, anise, or lemon, resulting in a delectable combination of flavors.

3. Marzipan is a delicious confection made from almonds and sugar. During the Christmas season, marzipan sculptures shaped like fruits, animals, and other festive themes are available.

4. Cava: Cava is Spain's sparkling wine, and it's ideal for toasting throughout the Christmas and New Year's holidays. It's frequently served with fresh fruits and snacks.

5. Pestiños are a honey-glazed pastry that is frequently connected with Andalusian cuisine. During the holiday season, they are sweet, sticky, and seductive.

7.4 Dining Recommendations

When it comes to Christmas dining in Alicante, you're spoiled for choice. Here are a few suggestions for unforgettable eating experiences:

1. El Portal Restaurant: Located in the heart of Alicante's old town, El Portal provides a charming

and personal eating experience. The restaurant is well-known for its innovative Spanish food, and its Christmas menu is a gourmet voyage through regional cuisines.

2. Cervecería Sento: Cervecera Sento is a popular neighborhood hangout for authentic Alicante cuisine. It's a great spot for fresh seafood and traditional cuisine.

3. El Xato: El Xato, located in nearby La Nucia, is famous for its Pavo Trufado, making it a must-visit for anyone looking for this seasonal delicacy.

4. El Esturión Restaurant: Located along the Explanada de Espana, El Esturión offers a one-of-a-kind eating experience with views of the

Mediterranean. Fresh seafood and regional specialties are on the menu.

5. Taberna del Gourmet: This Michelin-starred restaurant in the center of Alicante serves traditional Spanish meals with a modern touch. It's a great option for a memorable Christmas meal.

6. Restaurant L'Escaleta: Located in the nearby village of Cocentaina, L'Escaleta is renowned for its imaginative and exquisite food and offers a Michelin-starred dining experience.

Alicante's eating scene provides something for everyone, whether you're looking for classic Spanish meals, regional specialties, or innovative culinary inventions. During the holiday season, the city's restaurants are decked out in festive decorations, creating a warm and inviting environment for holiday dining.

8. SHOPPING FOR SOUVENIRS

8.1 Unique Christmas Gifts from Alicante

Souvenir shopping in Alicante is a lovely experience, especially during the Christmas season when the city comes alive with festive markets and one-of-a-kind gift possibilities. Here are some suggestions for one-of-a-kind Christmas gifts to bring back from your Alicante vacation:

1. Turron: Turron is a traditional Christmas food in Spain and makes a fantastic gift. There are a range of flavors available, ranging from basic almond to chocolate-covered and unique innovations.

2. Wine & Drinks: Spain is well-known for its high-quality wines and drinks. Consider a bottle of local wine or Horchata Liqueur, a typical Spanish drink made from tiger nuts.

3. Saffron is a prized spice used in Spanish cooking. It's a one-of-a-kind and scented present for folks who enjoy cooking and culinary excursions.

4. Alicante is well-known for its pottery, and you can get everything from colorful plates to classic Spanish kitchenware. These make lovely and handy souvenirs.

5. Esparto Grass Products: Esparto grass is a natural fabric that has traditionally been utilized in Spanish handicrafts. Baskets, bags, and home decor made with esparto grass are available.

6. Handcrafted Jewelry: Local jewelry businesses sell one-of-a-kind creations that reflect Alicante's culture and workmanship. Consider one-of-a-kind creations fashioned from semi-precious stones or local materials.

7. Local Artwork: Alicante is a mecca for artists, and you can find a wide range of local artwork around the city, including paintings, sculptures, and crafts that express the beauty and character of the region.

8.2 Artisan Markets and Boutiques

Alicante's artisan markets and boutiques provide a variety of one-of-a-kind and locally created things, making them ideal for souvenir shopping. Here are a few locations to visit:

1. Mercado Central: Located in the heart of Alicante, this bustling market is a wonderful place to explore local food products such as fresh vegetables, spices, and handmade cheeses. It also sells one-of-a-kind cookware, olive oils, and handcrafted ceramics.

2. Mercado de Navidad: Alicante's Christmas market, Mercado de Navidad, is a must-see during the holiday season. You'll discover a large variety of seasonal gifts, decorations, and crafts here, making it ideal for picking up Christmas-themed souvenirs.

3. Casa Carbonell: Located in a historic structure along the Explanada de Espana, Casa Carbonell is a marketplace that sells a variety of things such as apparel, jewelry, and traditional Spanish fans. It

combines traditional and contemporary shopping experiences.

4. El Corte Inglés: Spain's largest department store sells everything from fashion and beauty to gadgets and gourmet foods. It's a one-stop shop for a variety of souvenirs.

5. Local Boutiques: There are various local boutiques and craft shops in Alicante that highlight the work of area artisans. Discover hidden gems by strolling through the streets of the old town and the surroundings surrounding Explanada de Espana.

6. If you're in Alicante on a Thursday, the Santa Faz Flea Market is a terrific place to find vintage

and antique items ranging from jewelry to furniture and collectibles.

8.3 Local Handicrafts

Alicante is well-known for its rich handcraft culture, and discovering these local items is a rewarding experience. Some examples of local handicrafts to watch out for are:

1. Esparto Grass Products: Esparto grass is a traditional material used to make a variety of goods ranging from bags and baskets to placemats and ornamental pieces. These handmade items encapsulate the soul of the region.

2. Ceramics: Alicante's ceramics are remarkable, with vivid colors and detailed designs. Decorative

plates, vases, and tiles that reflect the region's tradition can be found.

3. Traditional Embroidery: Spanish hand fans, known as "abanicos," are both functional and artistic. Fans made of silk, lace, and wood can be found, and they are frequently embellished with exquisite patterns and designs.

4. Local Textiles: The region is famed for its textiles, and you may find a variety of things that exhibit local workmanship, such as handwoven blankets, scarves, and carpets.

5. Traditional Embroidery: Skilled embroiderers in Alicante create stunning hand-embroidered textiles such as tablecloths, shawls, and apparel items.

6. Marble Products: The Alicante region is recognized for its marble production, and you can discover a variety of marble products, ranging from sculptures and vases to decorative pieces.

Consider the distinctive goods made by local artists when shopping for souvenirs in Alicante. These sculptures not only make thoughtful gifts, but they also contribute to the region's rich cultural legacy. Whether you visit artisan markets or boutique shops, you'll find a broad variety of unusual and lovely souvenirs to remind you of your Christmas vacation in Alicante.

9. ITINERARY AND DAY-TO-DAY GUIDE

9.1 Day 1: Arrival and City Orientation

Your Christmas break in Alicante starts with your arrival. Depending on your arrival time, you can check into your chosen lodging and freshen up. Consider the following activities for your first day to kickstart your journey:

- Orientation Stroll: Take a stroll along the Explanada de España, a lovely waterfront promenade surrounded by palm trees. This is an excellent area to take in the scenery and get a sense of the city.

- Santa Barbara Castle: Spend the afternoon at Santa Barbara Castle. The castle provides panoramic views of Alicante and is an excellent way to learn about the city's geography. You can take a lift up to the castle or walk up for a little adventure.

- Dinner: Dine at a local restaurant along the Explanada de Espana on your first night. As you enjoy your first evening in Alicante, try fresh seafood, paella, or traditional Spanish meals.

9.2 Day 2: Exploring the Old Town

Day 2 is dedicated to touring Alicante's ancient Old Town, where you will learn about its rich history and tradition. Here are some ideas to help you make the most of your day:

- Breakfast: Begin your day with a traditional Spanish breakfast at a neighborhood café. Try churros with hot chocolate or coffee and toast with tomato and olive oil.

- Alicante Old Town: Spend the morning walking through the Old Town's tiny alleyways and squares. Visit the Co-Cathedral of San Nicolás, the Basilica of Santa María, and the Town Hall.

- Lunch: In the Old Town, enjoy a classic Spanish meal at a small restaurant or tapas bar. Enjoy Gazpacho, pulpo a la Gallega, and other regional favorites.

- Post-Lunch Explorations: After lunch, stroll around the old streets, where you can discover small stores, boutiques, and hidden jewels.

- Dinner: Return to Old Town for a delectable meal at a local restaurant. Try typical Spanish meals while taking in the atmosphere of this ancient area.

9.3 Day 3: Christmas Markets and Culinary Delights

On Day 3, get into the holiday mood with Alicante's Christmas markets and culinary delights:

- Breakfast: Begin your day with a substantial breakfast at your hotel or a nearby café.

- Mercado de Navidad: Spend the morning exploring the Mercado de Navidad, a Christmas market. Find holiday presents, decorations, and refreshments.

- Lunch: Grab a bite to eat at a neighborhood restaurant or market stall. Try some local delicacies or street food.

- Culinary session in the Afternoon: Attend a culinary session to learn how to make traditional Spanish dishes or pastries. It's a pleasant and educational exercise that gives you a taste of Alicante's culinary culture.

- Dinner: Dine at a restaurant that serves a special Christmas cuisine in the evening. Traditional cuisine such as Pavo Trufado and local seafood selections are available.

9.4 Day 4: New Year's Eve Celebrations

As the New Year approaches, enjoy the exciting New Year's Eve activities in Alicante:

- Morning Relaxation: Spend a leisurely morning relaxing, possibly with a walk along the beach or a visit to a local spa.

- Lunch: Savor the Mediterranean flavors with a late lunch at a restaurant with a seaside outlook.

- New Year's Eve Planning: Spend the afternoon planning New Year's Eve celebrations. Consider joining the many residents who celebrate at home with family and friends.

- Midnight Countdown: Join the residents in one of the city's plazas or along the Explanada de España to celebrate the New Year with a spectacular fireworks show.

- New Year's Salute: After the clock strikes midnight, salute the New Year with Cava, Spanish sparkling wine, and possibly the 12 grapes for good luck.

9.5 Day 5: Epiphany Parade and Departure

Your last day in Alicante falls on the day of the Epiphany Parade, a joyous celebration:

- After a leisurely breakfast, check out of your lodgings. You can leave your luggage at the hotel and explore the city on your own.

- Cabalgata de los Reyes Magos: Watch the Epiphany Parade, Cabalgata de los Reyes Magos, as the Three Wise Men parade through the streets, throwing sweets to the crowds.

- Lunch: Before you go, treat yourself to a festive meal at a local restaurant.

- Departure: Gather your belongings and make your way to Alicante's airport or train station to begin your journey home, leaving with you fond memories of your Alicante Christmas vacation.

This day-by-day itinerary will help you make the most of your Christmas vacation in Alicante by allowing you to see the city's cultural, culinary, and festive highlights. From the historic Old Town to the colorful New Year's Eve celebrations, your trip to Alicante is sure to be memorable and fulfilling.

10. PRACTICAL INFORMATION

10.1 Health and Safety Tips

It is critical to ensure your health and safety while on holiday in Alicante. Here are some important pointers to remember:

1. COVID-19 Precautions: In Alicante, continue to monitor and adhere to the most recent COVID-19 rules and limits. This could include masking, social isolation, and immunization requirements.

2. Travel Insurance: It is recommended that you obtain comprehensive travel insurance that covers

medical emergencies, trip cancellations, and other unforeseen circumstances. Make sure you have copies of your insurance information on hand.

3. Sun protection: Alicante can be bright and pleasant even in the winter. To avoid sunburn, protect yourself from the sun by using sunscreen, sunglasses, and a hat.

4. Stay Hydrated: Even if the weather is cooler, remaining hydrated is critical. Carry a reusable water bottle with you and drink frequently, especially if you intend to be active.

5. Food and Water Safety: While Spanish cuisine is great, make sure to dine at reputable locations and follow food safety precautions. Stick to bottled

water, and when dining out, explore local delicacies rather than street cuisine.

6. Safe Exploration: While Alicante is typically safe, be aware of your valuables in crowded areas and be on the lookout for pickpockets. When not in use, use hotel safes to store valuables.

7. In case of a medical emergency, familiarize yourself with the locations of neighboring hospitals, clinics, and pharmacies. In Spain, the emergency number for medical assistance is 112.

10.2 Emergency Contacts

It is critical to have the following contact information on hand in case of an emergency during your trip:

1. Medical Emergencies: Dial 112, Spain's emergency hotline, for medical assistance.

2. In the event of a crime or if you require police assistance, dial 112.

3. Dial 112. To report a fire or seek fire department assistance, dial 112.

4. Consular Assistance: If you are a foreign traveler in need of assistance from your home country's consulate or embassy, find the relevant contact information for your consulate or embassy in Alicante before your journey.

10.3 Money Matters: Currency and Banking

Understanding the local currency and banking systems is essential for a trouble-free vacation to Alicante:

1. Currency: Spain's official currency is the Euro (EUR). To properly manage your costs, become acquainted with Euro denominations and exchange rates.

2. ATMs: ATMs are extensively available around Alicante, and major credit and debit cards can be used to withdraw Euros. Be mindful of your bank's potential overseas transaction fees and currency conversion expenses.

3. Currency Exchange: There are various currency exchange offices in Alicante, particularly in tourist areas. While this is helpful, keep in mind the conversion rates and taxes.

4. Major credit and debit cards are frequently accepted in restaurants, hotels, and retail establishments. Visa and MasterCard are more generally accepted, although American Express and Discover may be less so.

5. Tipping is traditional but not required in Spain. In restaurants, a standard tip is roughly 10%, and you can even round up the amount as a show of appreciation. Tipping is less common at pubs and cafes.

10.4 Useful Websites and Apps

Consider using the following websites and applications to enhance your trip experience in Alicante:

1. Google Maps: The Google Maps app is extremely useful for navigation, public transportation information, and discovering nearby attractions and restaurants.

2. Renfe Cercanías: The Renfe Cercanas app gives schedules and real-time information for regional train services if you plan to explore local towns by train.

3. Alicante Tourism Website: Access information about events, sights, and tourist services by visiting the official tourism website of Alicante.

4. SpanishDict: This program can translate Spanish phrases and words, making it easier to connect with native speakers.

5. XE Currency Converter: Use this app to keep track of currency exchange rates and easily convert prices to your currency.

6. Weather Apps: The weather in Alicante can change quickly, so check local weather apps for the most up-to-date forecasts during your trip.

10.5 Tourist Information Centers

There are various tourist information centers in Alicante where you may get maps, brochures, and help planning your trip:

1. Tourist Info Alicante: This major information center, located in Explanada de Espana, provides maps, event information, and general help.

2. Alicante Tourism Office at the Airport: At Alicante-Elche Airport, there is a tourist information desk where you can pick up city maps and brochures.

3. Tourist Information in Old Town: There are information booths in the Old Town where you

may acquire directions for touring the historic region.

4. Beach Information Centers: Information centers around beaches provide information about beach services and activities.

10.6 Transportation Options in Alicante

Several modes of transportation make it easy to navigate Alicante:

1. Tram: A modern tram system connects Alicante with adjacent cities and the seashore. It's an excellent means of transportation for exploring coastal locations.

2. Buses: The city has a well-developed bus system that services both urban and suburban routes. Buses are a cost-effective mode of transportation.

3. Taxis: Taxis can be hailed on the street or hired using applications in Alicante. Check that the taxi has a working meter and ask for a receipt after the ride.

4. Car Rentals: If you want to explore the surrounding area or have more freedom in your travels, renting a car is an option. There are numerous rental agencies both at the airport and throughout the city.

5. Bicycles: Alicante offers a bike-sharing system, and you may borrow bicycles to explore the city

and its coastline in an eco-friendly and scenic manner.

6. Walking: Alicante is a pedestrian-friendly city with several attractions within walking distance. Stroll along the promenades, explore the Old Town, or walk along the beaches.

10.7 Language Tips and Useful Phrases

While many people speak English in Alicante, especially in tourist areas, it is welcomed if you try to communicate in Spanish. Here are some phrases to remember during your visit:

Hello: Hola

Good morning: Buenos días

Good afternoon: Buenas tardes

Good evening: Buenas noches

Please: Por favor

Thank you: Gracias

Yes: Sí

No: No

Excuse me: Perdón / Disculpe

I don't understand: No entiendo

How much is this?: ¿Cuánto cuesta esto?

Where is...?: ¿Dónde está...?

I need help: Necesito ayuda

Restroom: Baño

Water: Agua

Food: Comida

English: Inglés

Using these frequent phrases and trying to learn some basic Spanish will improve your interactions with locals and make your trip even more pleasurable.

Your Christmas holiday in Alicante will be a smooth and enriching experience if you stay informed about health and safety, understand the local currency and transportation alternatives, and have a basic comprehension of the Spanish language. Enjoy your time discovering this wonderful Spanish city's cultural and culinary attractions!

11. ADDITIONAL TRAVEL TIPS

11.1 Weather and Packing Updates

Understanding the weather in Alicante and packing accordingly can considerably improve your vacation experience. Here are some pointers to help you keep prepared:

1. Weather Variability: Because the temperature in Alicante may be unpredictable, check the weather forecast a few days before your trip and plan accordingly. While winters are generally moderate, there may be some rain and chilly evenings. Layer your clothing, including a light jacket or sweater.

2. Comfortable Walking Shoes: Wear comfortable walking shoes for touring the city and its attractions. Consider tougher footwear if you intend to explore the countryside, especially if you intend to hike.

3. Electrical Adapters: Spain's electrical outlets are Type C and Type F, therefore pack the proper adapters for your electronic gadgets. The standard voltage is 230V with a frequency of 50Hz.

4. Reusable Water Bottle: Because Alicante has drinkable tap water, you can bring a reusable water bottle with you to replenish during your trip. This not only cuts down on plastic waste, but it also keeps you hydrated.

5. Consider packing a power bank for on-the-go charging to guarantee you always have a charged phone for navigation.

11.2 Local Etiquette and Customs

Respecting local customs and etiquette is vital for a pleasant and pleasurable vacation to Alicante. Here are some crucial items to remember:

1. Greetings: Among friends and relatives, Spaniards typically greet one other with a kiss on both cheeks. In more formal settings, a handshake is customary.

2. Tipping is recommended but not required in restaurants and bars. It is typical to tip 10% of the

cost, however, you might simply round up the sum.

3. Siesta: Many stores and companies close for a few hours in the afternoon for siesta (typically between 2 and 5 p.m.). Make a plan for your activities and meals.

4. Punctuality: Spaniards have a more relaxed attitude toward time. Expect appointments or events to begin slightly later than expected.

5. While most places allow casual wear, dressing more formally when visiting churches or premium restaurants is a display of respect. Beachwear should be worn just at the beach and not in the city center.

6. Cultural Sites: Dress modestly when visiting religious or historic places. Women, for example, should cover their shoulders, while men should refrain from wearing sleeveless shirts.

11.3 Traveling with Kids or Pets

If you're traveling with children or pets, keep the following points in mind to ensure a family-friendly and pet-friendly vacation:

1. Alicante Beaches: Many Alicante beaches are family-friendly, with shallow waters and kid-friendly amenities. Playa del Postiguet and Playa de San Juan are two popular choices.

2. Alicante has several family-friendly attractions, including the Marq Provincial Archaeological

Museum and Terra Natura, a wildlife and water park. Exploring the city's parks and promenades is also a fun way to keep kids entertained.

3. Beaches for Pets: If you're traveling with a pet, keep in mind that some beaches have dedicated pet-friendly zones. Popular options include Playa de Agua Amarga and Playa de Agua Caliente.

4. Pet-Friendly lodgings: Before reserving your lodgings, check to see if they are pet-friendly and familiarize yourself with their pet policies.

5. Local Parks: Take leisurely walks with your pet around city parks such as El Palmeral and La Ereta Park.

6. Veterinary Services: Learn about local veterinary clinics and emergency services in case your pet needs help.

11.4 Sustainability and Responsible Travel

When visiting any destination, sustainability and responsible travel habits are becoming increasingly crucial. There are various ways to reduce your environmental affect and support local communities in Alicante:

1. Recycling: There are recycling containers located around Alicante. Make an effort to sort your trash and recycle properly.

2. To lessen your carbon footprint, consider taking public transit, such as trams and buses, or exploring the city on foot or by bicycle.

3. Respect Natural Areas: If you intend to explore the region's natural beauties, practice appropriate outdoor ethics. Respect the native flora and fauna, stay on designated pathways, and avoid trash.

4. Support Local Businesses: To help the local economy, eat at local restaurants, buy souvenirs from local artists, and stay in locally owned motels.

5. Water Conservation: Due to the possibility of water shortages in Alicante, use water wisely in your accommodations and while out and about.

You may make your stay in Alicante more enjoyable, respectful of local cultures, and environmentally responsible by keeping these additional travel recommendations in mind. Make the most of your Christmas break in this wonderful Spanish city by discovering its rich culture and scenic beauty.

12. CONCLUSION

Finally, your Christmas vacation in Alicante provides an enthralling mix of cultural riches, festive celebrations, and natural beauty. You'll make lasting memories as you explore the ancient Old Town, stroll along the lovely promenades, sample the local food, and participate in traditional Christmas activities.

The warm winter weather in Alicante provides a welcoming setting for visitors, and the city's coastline position provides options for outdoor activities and leisure. The city's bustling Christmas markets, the grandeur of Old Town, and the excitement of the Epiphany Parade all combine to provide a memorable holiday experience.

Make the most of your trip in Alicante by planning ahead of time, remaining informed about health and safety, respecting local customs, and being conscious of environmental effects. You can relish the beauty of Alicante in this way, departing with a heart full of fantastic experiences and keepsakes that encapsulate the character of this Spanish gem.

Whether you're traveling with family, and friends, or on a solitary adventure, Alicante will make your 2023 Christmas season memorable. Enjoy the sights, sounds, and flavors of this wonderful destination while making memories to last a lifetime.

Printed in Great Britain
by Amazon

34337004R00064